Unspent Possibilities

Poetry of Light and Shade

I0104032

Jennifer Syrkiewicz

chipmunkapublishing

the mental health publisher

Jennifer Syrkiewicz

Published by

Chipmunkapublishing

PO Box 6872

Brentwood

Essex CM13 1ZT

United Kingdom

http://www.chipmunkapublishing.com

Edited by Regi Pilling

Cover image by Jim Poyner Photography, York

Chipmunkapublishing gratefully acknowledge the support of Arts Council England.

Unspent Possibilities

This volume of poetry is dedicated to Joan Williams, who lit up a straight path through the darkness

Jan Read who always accompanied me upon it

and the somewhat darker memory of Alexandra Gail Darvill

Jennifer Syrkiewicz

Author Biography

Jennifer Syrkiewicz has been writing all her life, drawing from a mixture of personal experience and imagination to inform her fiction.

Diagnosed with Bipolar Affective Disorder, Jennifer wrote her first novel, 'Gardening in the Dark', to raise awareness of the condition and express how Bipolar affects the lives of both the person diagnosed, and those around them. Since writing the novel, Jennifer has set up a support group for the condition in her area.

Jennifer was born in 1976, in Yorkshire. Following a meandering trail across the UK to attend various universities, she is now happily settled in North Yorkshire with her husband Paul and two dogs. She runs a small Communications business and spends most of her time blogging, writing articles and producing fiction and poetry.

Jennifer Syrkiewicz

Unspent Possibilities

Contents

From the man you left

Tonight

Elegy

Christina the Astonishing

Much better, now.

The serpent

One day

This is just to say...

The red dress.

For my husband, who loves me anyway.

A one-way love affair

A flickering light

For Boudicca

Monday, after the rain.

Marshalling hope

Ungrounded

I am sorry

Up and away

The eye

Monday morning

You have been written about before

Unspent Possibilities

On politeness

Eternal sleep

For Damien

The song of the manic depressive

Half-life

There, but for the grace

Commuter hour

On nihilism

A fate worse

Tainted

Like wine

Seven thirty in the room of horrors

Two seasons in one year

On hope

Lament

The oldest questions

My handful of cells

Clinical Immunodermatology

Send

Transference

Pause and think of me

Freud revisited

Thorn Cross

You know who you are

Everything still the same

Unspent Possibilities

Something new has been created

A blue-tinged morning

Like an open mouth

With stripes of light

Streaking softly to the floor.

This is a fresh beginning;

It is conception

The point when two things

Join in union and create.

With ragged breath

Pulling life inwards

And a stretching reach

Towards the sun.

Jennifer Syrkiewicz

Breathing 101

A proud day, a day which stands erect and flushed with success

Whispering its prowess in to the wind.

I learned how to crawl today, one hesitant trembling knee placed

Inelegantly before the other.

Is there a certificate? A diploma? A graduation cap with tilted corners

Reaching for the sky?

This is my post-graduate reward – one crawling inch closer

Towards living again.

Chasing Apollo

Can you hear me? Can you?

Cease dancing for a second, to the tune which only

You and I can hear.

Pause in your frivolity, Prince

Look downwards if you dare and catch a quiet glimpse

Of one who would be you.

My reflection

Tonight, remember this.

You haven't seen, again, the full cycle of the moon turn in to an orb of silver.

You have forgotten the sweet smell of fresh-cut luscious grass, dipped in dew.

You have the chance to bite in to a plump ripe nectarine, and feel the sensuous

Juice run through your fingers, like possibilities. Like sun-blood. Like warm cider.

Remember this, tonight.

Somebody, somewhere, one of your future people are looking through a rain-smudged

Window, smiling slightly as she thinks of you; your laugh, your quirks and irritations.

A person you are yet to meet is walking through puddles, unconsciously waiting to

Graze your elbow and turn and smile and for one small perfect moment, connect.

Unspent Possibilities

Do not let yourself forget.

Soon you will be a shining. The warm sun in your hair will push the scent of yourself

Upwards and outwards and you will occupy your space with grace and surety. You.

You will look upwards and see a shooting star, and make a wish. Perhaps you will

Trip and fall and see your vivid life blood run from your bruise. A necessary reminder.

Jennifer Syrkiewicz

Come quickly

Hurry, sunshine.

Inexorable time is dragging across the floor like a lame dog, a black dog.

A shadowed corpse of betrayal and lost hope.

Hurry, dawn.

Push through and do what you do best, in all your simplicity.

Unspent Possibilities

A long-standing problem

Yes, Freud, it is all in the womb.

A canker screeching like a harpy.

Look at me! My breasts! My groin!

See how the oestrogen runs rampant

Across the parallels of the body.

Observe the abject insanity of female

Maladies – Fat, ugly, inept, ashamed.

(So ashamed, and growing more so as

The ripples of hysteria prompt a vast

Abyss to open out in lush flourishes)

The questions which haunt your lips

Will also be present upon our own.

Why does this happen? Blame the

Sumptuous undulating curves, and the

Perennial need to be mother, daughter,

Whore. (Always, secretly, the whore).

Legs spread akimbo in the grasping

Surface of temporary satisfaction. The

Corporeal carping of unfulfillment.

Laughing too loudly as the battlefield

Of womanhood opens its sucking maw

And lets us in, to shriek and wail and

Possibly, sometimes, stand in awe at

The beauty of everything we are.

Unspent Possibilities

Parting the rushes

Today I think I may get up very early and then dress in a bright orange jumper that has threads of starlight in it and then run or dance down the curving stairs through to the kitchen and then perhaps it may be time to clean or sing from my stomach along to the radio even if I don't know the words, because my words will be right from me and my soul and not yours and then perhaps afterwards

I think I will definitely run for a while until the rhythm of my feet lifts me off the ground and when I stretch my arms out I can feel myself flying and then afterwards, so soon, so sweet, I will decide it is certainly time to become a ballet dancer just for a few minutes and so my body will shrink and stretch taut and lean and I will pirouette and bend like pulled elastic and then snapping back in to a former place

I will agree that surely it is time to read to listen learn and so I will order myriad books on all different subjects in the hope of very soon becoming a poet, a priest, a practitioner, project manager, a business! An empire! A possibility and then when the brain has cavorted over the pages like a lost thing for a while I will begin to create and this is a time of music and words which twist together in perfect circles and the edges will run away without me for a while and perhaps afterwards I will certainly agree that it is time to change everything and in quick succession I will become a blonde a brunette a biker chick a baritone and perhaps just a nothing with infinite possibility and we could make love and your breath will be lost with the beauty of it all and when we move together you will see stars and I will be a puppeteer making the starlight so bright we have to shield our eyes the music will be playing quieter and then louder like a secret soundtrack can you hear? Can you hear now? Nownownownownownownow? and this my body, perfect in every way and ever obliging will be able to dance wilder and wilder and more and more bright until I am the only thing in the universe, or perhaps a little bigger, so brimming with unspent possibilities, today.

Unspent Possibilities

Possibilities

When I was little, I wanted to grow up to be.

Unspent Possibilities

Possibilities

When I was little, I wanted to grow up to be.

Kicking up leaves

What happens if, suddenly, you lose who you are?

You find yourself, your body, walking down some

street one morning, with the wind kicking up leaves

and sunlight fighting to come through the trees.

You are walking to an internal rhythm which you don't

recognise to be your own. A different beat thrums.

You don't stray from the path, your body speaks for you,

hunching its shoulders against the breeze, pursing its

lips on a taut cold face, wearing a protective expression

to face the world. Inside, the bit which you would have

recognised, the thoughts, snippets of music and internal

dialogue, is gone. This then, is what you are.

A body without mind, an empty vessel, as each thought
is

battened down and refused acknowledgement the
second

it tries to surface, because the 'I' that you once were,

can no longer afford to acknowledge it.

Unspent Possibilities

Enduring

There had been times when she had felt love like agony, like destruction.

She fell in love quietly, viciously. She loved like acid in her stomach,

Tearing her insides asunder.

She loved like sleepless nights, like hypnotic visions, hallucinations. She loved like the craving for a certain scent.

She loved with heady, reckless, silent abandon.

She yielded herself up to him like the first woman, in a time before cynicism and experience had tainted the romance of Shakespeare, the mystical lyricism of Keats.

Before romance, as the saying went, was dead.

Love was wide open, daring him to fall inside.

It was forgiving and clouded and immediate, a warmth spreading, a smile blooming secretly behind a covered mouth.

It was everything, sometimes.

Consuming, desperate, all-encompassing.

Love like the sea, like the infinite possibilities of the stars.

Love such as she had dreamed about, dragging her heels through her teenage years,

watching Hollywood portrayals of what idealised love could actually attain.

She loved like hunger. Like death.

This clawing sensuality, the blushing and fumbling and thirst soon faded.

With the inevitability of time, it ebbed away and left...

nothing. A heart-shaped hole. A half.

Unspent Possibilities

Accidental memories

A light went out, it pitched

A solitary smile in to darkness.

You cared for a while, I know

I think you cared for a short while?

And I recall a time when you gave your vows,

And I think back now, when the radio,

Blares out a stepped seventh,

And I turn and catch your secret smile,

And wonder where you are right now.

Just to touch your face, to make

Something new: an accidental memory.

Snapped like a twig, I'll share myself with him

And I would love the opportunity, if only once, to understand the question in him.

He is, like me, alone. I scrutinise his beautiful face sometimes, try and penetrate

behind those steel blue irises to understand what lies beneath.

I still don't know. I am still unsure, even as I finish his sentence for him, or

laugh at a joke because I can anticipate the punch line, what he is thinking.

Sometimes I catch him staring at me, too.

I know he is trying to fathom out the thoughts which run through my mind in an endless cacophony.

Sometimes we can tell each other what we are thinking, exactly as it happens.

We will hum the same snatch of song which has been belting out like an orchestra in the rooms of our mind, ricocheting around the cavities and hollows of our brains.

Unspent Possibilities

I will question whether he caught the tune from me,

Or whether I have hummed it into his mind so he picks it up, subconsciously.

Jennifer Syrkiewicz

Fear

Shame (a naked body, a gaze, a reluctant secret)

Love and hate do not require an explanation.

Fear. A creaking floorboard in the middle of the night.

The cautious opening of a door.

Fear as a well-travelled corner of a ceiling, with spider webs

tracing patterns in zig zags back and forth.

Damp fear. Hot fear. Silent and shamed fear.

Broken sleep, haunted dreams fear.

Fear, a silent secret that sits quietly like a coiled reptile in

the pit of the stomach, concealed from discovery.

My body, reassured, hums quietly, in the middle of the day with

the curtains drawn and the mattress squealing rhythmically to itself.

It is enough.

Unspent Possibilities

Grasping at Stars

Today she is a goddess, ethereal and sparkling with life -

Brimming in her fingertips; dancing in her eyes -

She runs, and the wind runs with her, lifting her beyond all reach.

Omnipotent, she soars skyward, stretching up

Like a balloon, billowed in a soft rubber breath -

Like a firework she soars and shimmers in light.

Run with her, although her light dazzles and her thoughts

Trip and twist in eddying, dizzying, sickening turns.

Laugh into the shadows when she smiles, catch this time,

For tomorrow her sheen may fade and she'll forget to smile.

The journal entries

These dreams are beautiful things,

Soft-glowing and illustrative,

Owned and claimed.

Sometimes I listen to them.

Sometimes they push me away.

Unspent Possibilities

All about you

I can feel the push of us making love.

In bright white shock that I feel at all.

It wasn't much; it wasn't much.

I would have lain down,

But you couldn't reach it all

Until my voice left me wordless

And you laughed like a thief,

Gathering swag, ready to run.

The first breath, the stretch

It begins in a brown room with purple curtains

It begins at an age where a thousand memories are blurred and distilled

In to one sharp intake of breath

Small fingers, sitting by the wall. A song

The lilac curtains.

When it is dark the patterns take on the form of ghoulish faces, rows of malevolent heads with different expressions.

They watch what goes on in the room,

And are watched in return by the girl who occupies the bed.

Unspent Possibilities

After the door has slammed shut

New love should be easy to walk away from.

Nothing really given, nothing truly taken,

just the burgeoning hope of potential, the

half-truth before knowledge eclipses romance.

The forgiveness which comes from not knowing

someone, hopefulness stemming from the desire to

believe, or suspend disbelief. The broadening of

narrow horizons into understanding. There is very little

Truth to be found in new love. This, I do not heed.

I trust myself to fall, unchecked, in to the new potential.

Jennifer Syrkiewicz

Memory Box

A recess behind the curtain, clamped down tight

A little wooden box, crammed with soft memories

A smooth pebble, worn by the tide, dimmed and dry.

A handful of photographs capturing smiles on to canvas.

A feather dropped by some wide-winged bird by the sea.

A reminder, scrawled on a scrap, that things evolve, move.

A sixpence crammed in to a cork, heralding our futures

An order of service, a crystal prism gathering dust,

A book, a poem, a picture, a bottled scent, a promise.

With these gathered thoughts and dreams, an entire

Army can be felled simply by opening the rusting lid.

Unspent Possibilities

From the man you left

It has been consummated;

That which nothing mortal,

Nothing ethereal, can sever,

Nor human platitudes divide.

Tonight

Damn everything, tonight.

Damn the people whom I trust,

And who won't listen.

Damn the rain.

Damn the river of doubt

Which flows through each

Compartment of my life

And drowns it.

Unspent Possibilities

Elegy

My Father discarded her.

Sometimes she baked cakes, sang songs with laughing lyrics. Sometimes she cleaned the house, though not very often.

Elated, she'd fly in the wind.

Depressed, she dissolved.

She hurt us with finesse.

She drank herself to death. The alcohol in her bloodstream, the futility of her. I loved her and hated her.

And now I capture and cage her.

Now she is mainly untraceable.

I find her in a picture, a song.

A scent, or in my own white face with the large lips and turned-up nose. I catch her when he looks at me with scorn.

I see her reflection in his eyes.

Sometimes, she is lost.

Jennifer Syrkiewicz

Christina the Astonishing

Christina Mirabilis, I know you

With your excessive torment

Your talk of hell and heaven

Dipping a frenzied toe in to the

Rushing wilds of insanity.

They did not understand.

They were afraid of your whipped

Tongue, afraid to hear your words

Because, after all, are we not just

One solitary step behind you?

Christina, patron saint of madness

I see you in my dreams.

Twisting and turning and fitting,

Writhing against the terrible truth

Of life. We are all, each one of us,

Unspent Possibilities

Mad. Did they charge you like

A flattened battery? Did they

Hold you down and speak at you

Until your brain shifted and cried

Out in lonely confusion?

Or, sweet lunatic, did they stand

In a circle of awe and hear the prophesy

Of civilisation, understanding that

You were one dancing step behind

Eternal realisation, eternal truth?

Much better, now.

Oh, hello. It's you again.

I remember you.

The surge, the upsurge.

Naturally, as I am far superior

To any other human being,

On a secret mission of genius,

Universally popular and adored

With a quiet acknowledgment of my own

Superiority...

I recognise you, old friend.

You are the power that gives me wings

That makes me fly that little bit higher

Than everyone else.

Looking down,

At insignificant things

And laughing, safe in scorn.

I missed you , when I was crawling.

Unspent Possibilities

I missed you when everything was dark.

Now I understand that all along

I was just waiting, again.

Waiting and watching for my own

Undiscovered omnipotence.

The serpent

Not long away, like a serpent coiled in expectation, you wait

Gnawing at stomach linings and intestines, shifting and turning.

You feed off fear. You are fear's sister, thriving and growing strong

On half-formed thoughts of desperation and the unknown.

I know you. I remember your forked tongue and scaled back

And the way you jump with glee, causing trepidation.

What am I afraid of? The sun tumbling from the sky? War?

An unseen cancer feasting on cells, waiting to be discovered?

Certainly not death. Perhaps life. Perhaps, like so many before,

I am simply afraid of you, grey serpent. The fear of fear itself.

Unspent Possibilities

One day

I will stand up very tall

and admit myself to the world.

But not today.

Jennifer Syrkiewicz

This is just to say...

I have taken

the tablets

that were in

the pill box

and which

you were probably

hiding

for safety.

Forgive me

they were important

so sweet

and so final.

Unspent Possibilities

The red dress

I looked down and the dress had taken on my form,
its secrets across my hips and thighs. It was a bold
and remarkable dress. A dress that promised to get
an uneven life back on to a square footing.

A dress that colluded with me quietly,
snaking across all the parts of my body that
made me a woman and pledging to guide me.
With this dress on, I would be bold and proud.

With this dress, I was not a pure white girl, but
a reckless and unashamed woman. The dress sighed
across my arms, the long sleeves and tapering cuffs
slipping down until they clothed me.

There was no flesh to be revealed under this dress,
but it promised promiscuity and future misdemeanors.
It was provocatively, teasingly, perfect. It clothed me in

Jennifer Syrkiewicz

Sighs of silk like a transparent, protective cocoon.

Unspent Possibilities

For my husband, who loves me anyway

This, now.

This is my place in time.

If I stretch my arms high enough, I can sweep the sky for stars.

If I bend down low, so low,

I can plunge my fist into the womb of the earth.

I used to be small, bunched and afraid.

This, now.

This is where I claim my shuddering self.

Back.

I will fling their useless words to the winds.

I will look deep inside and pull out the darkness

And feed it into the dank earth.

Where these seeds are buried,

A tree will grow.

The tree will become a copse

The copse a forest. The forest a new world.

Here I will run with my open heart outstretched, open

To receive a new beginning.

This, now.

This is my place in time.

I am alive. I am nourished and sturdy and open and free.

This. (I am loved; I love)

Now.

Unspent Possibilities

A one-way love affair

...and the thirst, which is creeping over me

(even as I sit there in the blue chair in the white

 room with a blue carpet, with the heater pumping

 out inadequate fumes and he of the sharpened face

watching me, writing things down with a downturned

mouth and eyes which shout out all my multitude of
dank

inadequacies and look down from above while deciding
my

fate like Pilate and his predictable thumb because he is
whole

and lissome and alive and I am dragged mumbling and
cursing to

myself when they have decreed that it is time to move or
breathe or

shit or eat or talk or scratch or wake up in the middle of
the night drenched

in fear of what lies ahead because the one single lifeline
of nothingness has been

erased just as surely as if they had stripped me naked and pulled my soul from the

machine and left me hanging like so much meat on a sharpened hook in preparation

for the curing, the cure, which involves as ever a period of suspension without liquid and

this is drying out in which the hide toughens and the last vestiges of liquid are squeezed from

eyes which shed everything before them in a little pool because soon I will be ready to devour)

Unspent Possibilities

A flickering light

The cylindrical honeyed tallow, the soft wick,

which begins unblemished, but ignites into a

sulphurous flickering fuse. The flame, casting a

halo of light in an orb around its centre. Responsive,

amber, with the centre marked out in a blue leaf,

the light issuing from it. Heat as a secondary attribute,

the one which is often forgotten as we gaze transfixed

at the centre of the dancing, flickering orange flame.

Best of all of the candles' qualities lies in the centre pool,

the hot mouldable wax that flows like tears down the smooth

shaft, cooling into stalactites. It runs unchecked, until the

laws of physics slow it, harden it. The centre pool is irresistible,

pulling you in, taunting you with its warmth, begging to be

touched, dipped in to. Candles remind us of everything we most

revere and fear. Death lies in their centre, memories of brooding

chapels and released prayers.

That something which can dispel darkness should be so associated with

death. Candles hold memories in their smooth forms, squat and round

or slim, lean memories. Churches, weddings, blackouts, stories narrated

in low voices across a sphere of light. The smell, at once warm and acrid,

is an anchor in the mind of a myriad conflicting memories. We reach out

tentative fingers and touch, mould the wax. Effigies, ritual, black magic and

God lie in the centre, calling for us to respond and grasp it, if we can only

navigate beyond the fire, the flame.

Unspent Possibilities

For Boudicca

I will throw my arms up into the wind and lift my head high,

higher than the victors of this battle.

I will scream my freedom into the faces of these animals, and prove to them

one last time that an Iceni Queen is not afraid of death.

I will celebrate this day as a glorious battle, a testament to kinship and

loyalty. The vial around my neck is burning my skin,

reminding me that there is always an alternative to the destiny

that they have mapped out for me. I will claim my own life.

With sweet poison, I dare them to steal my last breaths from me.

I will drink the draught deeply, charged in the belief that

my husband awaits, and my daughters will be sure to follow shortly.

We will meet again and continue our journey, blessed by the gods,

Leave this land to the Romans. We no longer have a place here, on this

battle ground, with death and the stench of blood permeating every breath

and leaving an acrid sting in the throat. I am coming for you, now. I am coming.

I will hold my arms up to receive the sky.

Unspent Possibilities

Monday, after the rain.

Beginning afresh is like being born again

Tasting a sharp lemon for the first time

Testing things. The acrid sweetness of

Burning debris behind, the sweet and slightly

Salt newness of breathing to be found.

It is like stepping out in to unmarked sand

Washed smooth as glass by the tide.

Like hesitating before the first dive in

To pure, unrippled water. It is the scent

Of an uncreased spine. It is beautiful.

Like an unchecked ascent through the clouds

With unused eyes, gazing at the horizon

And calculating how far one would have to

Fly to arrive there. It is the feel of hot breath

Upon a shivering neck, and enclosing arms.

Marshalling hope

You are two shards of sunlight, intertwined

Carrying light like the hermit holding his lamp aloft

Casting your brightness in to the dark corners of the world

In search of new possibilities.

You are kindness; the kindness found in a maternal glance

Or a fatherly squeeze of a clammy small hand,

Or the smile on the face of a child held aloft

Above the crowds of consternation.

You are my dream fulfillment, with your quiet

Words of understanding, your reassuring quirks

And infinite acceptance. I love you, as only a

Broken thing can love the whole.

Unspent Possibilities

Ungrounded

I am below you, sometimes,

Sometimes clawing at broken desiccated earth

With fingernails chipped and stained from the swoop

Of last week's parties.

Sometimes, I am above.

Looking down, triumphantly from a pedestal

Of pure self belief. Venus, Me. Aphrodite of

A womb lined with gilt.

When you ask if I hear voices

I am regretful. "No." I state firmly, with no

Echo. I wish, I wish that I sometimes did

Hear other, more sparkling, conversations.

I am sorry

I apologise

For trying to take my own life, which does not belong to me

For making you frightened, so that you cry at night as I lie in a heap, in a corner, on a ward.

For the selfishness which binds me up in my self, unable to see how I am hurting you more each time.

I am sorry

For lashing out at you, my beautiful and caring friend

Who stands safe and strong as I am buffeted by fear, by sadness, by death, by death.

Who refuses to turn away when the darkness fills the room like a bunker, as an everlasting night.

Forgive me

For eating away at your consciousness until I fill your entire mind

For cavorting at the edges of insanity like a child playing with a naked flame

Unspent Possibilities

For sometimes being the flame, my self, dancing and growing taller and higher and ever more blue.

Jennifer Syrkiewicz

Up and away

Yes! We are going to the coast

Or perhaps the cinema, theatre.

For a drive, a walk, a run, a drink?

May we cook something, dine out,

Dine in, eat off the sparkling body

Of the other? Or can we please,

Paint something, draw something,

Sketch something, become still

Life, but not so still, and stretch

And fly and dream and laugh so

Hard our sides split and breath spills

Out upon the floor? Can we climb

Somewhere high, a hill, a church,

A mountain and look down at the

Tiny people below who look like bugs

Wandering aimlessly, pointlessly,

Gazing up in awe in the face of our

Unspent Possibilities

Sheer effervescent brilliance?

The eye

You are beautiful, she said,

And the words hugged close

Like a favourite cardigan.

Beautiful. A thing which radiates

Light and life, like a glowing

Ember kicked from a campfire.

I laughed. Turn me inside out,

I wanted to say. I am as scarred

And deformed as relentless death.

Unspent Possibilities

Monday morning

In the village, this morning, the baker sits with his grandchild

on his knee, bouncing the child in to a new week

The cobbler leans on the door of his hut, smoking cigarettes

Watching a dog announcing his presence to the world.

A battered car pulls in to the side of the wide road

And a woman with a perfect face climbs out

To visit the hairdressers, where black towels lined

Up like flags swing in the breeze, drying out.

The wind catches empty fallen leaves and swirls

them in to eddying patterns of mould-mulch brown and

orange, a kaleidoscope. Clashing with the grey

steel sky and the threat of sudden mean-spirited rain.

People crouch in houses, wondering sometimes

What today will bring. A laugh, a smile, a heady

Argument which leads to frenzied sex? A knock

On the door, a siren, a handful of pills, a tear.

Unspent Possibilities

You have been written about before

Marilyn, a name like a peal of church bells

Heralding a new union.

A blonde curl falling over an eye in tears.

An outside, an inside,

A gasp of thrusting pain and a sharp cry.

Analysis. Truth and deceit.

You are legendary, in your white dress, the

Sudden gust of wind.

So frail and broken, even the harsh sweeping

Eye of the camera

Can read your palms and tell you what you are.

On Politeness

For just one day, imagine if we

Could speak our minds aloud

To set our miserly spirits free

And alienate the crowd.

To answer 'how are you'

With a roll of the eyes; a sigh

And if we felt entirely blue,

Quietly begin to cry.

Much easier to be sullen, to sulk

To tell the trappings of truth,

To be mean-spirited and skulk,

Or sarcastic, alone and aloof

Picture the scene of turmoil;

The arched and terrified look

Unspent Possibilities

How people would recoil,

From the courage that it took.

Eternal sleep

Lock me in a white room, with the windows barred and all material removed

Chain me now; drug me in to a stupor so deep it feels like the unknown,

Where I cannot dream, can only breathe a steady rhythm, and lie and wait

For the light to come creeping and shifting through the crevices and cracks.

Tie the cyclical thoughts down in the hollows of my weary mind, and

Scrub this malodorous body clean, wiping away the white-pill cold scent of

Failure and the grubbing bleak dank sadness which oozes from these pores,

Gaping and gushing forth their sorrow, their solitude, their endless weariness.

This will pass, I know. And yet, while the clock hands seem to tick backwards

Unspent Possibilities

As time creeps and drags its heels with mocking light movements, and the light

On the wall sweeps ever backwards instead of pulling the heavy world onwards,

It is hard to remember that this is insignificant, that it will soon change; improve.

Not without hope, the skin still shrinks back from coldness, from heat, reacting

To stimuli as the mind sleeps on. The body still stretches and demands sustenance,

Angrily growling and complaining in an effort to be fed and watered. The bowels shift,

The head nods, demanding sleep. It understands life in a way I cannot. This will pass.

Jennifer Syrkiewicz

For Damien

Your eyes, piercing blue and jumping with soul stains

And that bored, deliciously cruel mouth, hiding

Vampire teeth and hunger, why do you sing? Sing to me?

The words, underpinned by minor chords which

Slash the smile off unsuspecting faces, speak of a

Sorrow deeper than any gully. You are lost, spinning and-

Placing these notes down upon half-torn jagged

Papers and collecting them as the harpy collects

Cries of sadness, twisting and turning some magic spell,

Three times this way, three times that, you wave your

Hand across the song and soul wracking sorrow

Ensues. You are my dark secret, the one whose music I crave.

Unspent Possibilities

The song of the manic depressive

Drifting through life with a

Quiet certitude that we will

soon die, soon escape our flesh, yet -

There is still hope; always hope

like a knife point, sharpened

And honed in order to protect and

Defend against the cloth-black night.

For, after all, are we not gifted

In our creativity and wry look at

Life? This is the truth. This is

Our song of joy, of sorrow, of life.

Half-life

It is evening, and the darkness steals under the curtains

Painting the edges with musty impenetrable grey.

People go to their houses and wait for the light to return.

It is night, and blackness swoops from the sky and invades

Open snoring mouths, choking and muffling

While a handful of restless souls steal glances at clock faces.

It is morning, and the sun clambers upwards to shed light

Across tired faces, goading them to work again

As flowers unfurl to greet the sudden dazzle, the warmth.

It is afternoon, and we are poised again to watch the

Inevitable crawl of time across our pages, stolen

Unspent Possibilities

From books, from which the last page has been ripped and torn.

Jennifer Syrkiewicz

There, but for the grace

On the other side of this wall, a lonely

Woman sits and weaves cottons in to

A vast tapestry of tears, deep colours

Of Autumn gathered in intricate knots

And garnished with bitterness; sorrow.

Still smarting at seventy, she cries hotly

Because her daddy gave her away when

She was just seven; too frightened to state

That her heart cracked and won't heal.

She sighs for the broken, scarred little girl.

Fruitless, now, barren with solitude,

Her children lost to her, afraid to hold out

Their chubby arms and admit that they

Loved her anyway, she has extracted her

Punishment upon then, unwittingly.

Unspent Possibilities

Closed to our world, stitching out time

With trembling hands, she waits for the

Day when the sorrow will freeze and the

Tears will dry, and life is exhaled in a single,

Desperate, banal and forgotten long sigh.

Jennifer Syrkiewicz

Commuter hour

No rush, now. Sitting over tepid tea

And a half-drawn cigarette, and smoke.

Someone is playing an aria, so sad;

Pulling the universe in to today.

People meander in twos and threes

All in a hurry to move to another place.

The table, round and uncompromising

As an anchor, coated in ash like lichen,

And the chair suspended; safe. There is

Nowhere to be but here, right now.

There is nowhere important to go.

You have just left me, and still, in light

A smile plays upon my tea-stained lips.

Unspent Possibilities

On Nihilism

So heady and attention-seeking, this jump

Downwards. So predictably self-centred,

Even if the self is simply, now, a blubbering void,

The full stretch of kohl-smudged damp sleep.

Letting go feels real; falling backwards and

Drowning in destructive pity which gnaws on

Angled limp limbs and encourages absolute

Lethargy. Like sustenance; like hot fresh tears.

Pounding upon the will to live, bleeding as

A fist full of splinters on a solid oak door.

Delicious, warm and hazy sorrow reaching

In to a bleak black chasm of pointlessness.

A Fate Worse

The sustenance goes down;

Spoonfuls of energy, processed

And then out; depleted.

This is positive. It keeps us,

The subjects, the impatients,

Alive. The alternative is that

For which we are blamed, if

We dare to contemplate it.

If this has to be done, this

Endless cycle of eating, and

Drinking, and breathing, I

Suddenly understand how

Madness sometimes expresses

Itself by taking the sufferers

Hand, grasping the stuff of life,

And smearing it over the walls.

Unspent Possibilities

Tainted

Look out, I'm off again. Stand back.

It's contagious, this pock-riddled

Lunacy I carry within me, as a worn

Horse bears a load, moving only when

Flogged, gasping and faltering along.

If you sneer, you with the curled lip

And the superiority complex which

Your doting mother bestowed upon

You when you learned to shit in a pot,

Clapping and blushing with pride...

I will open my babbling mouth and

Exhale upon you, and a host of horrors

Such as hysteria, hellfire and delusions

Of grandeur will coil outwards and claim

You, leaving you rocking and weary.

Like wine

This low is seductive, reaching out

Familiar gnarled arms and beckoning

With a welcoming toothless maw.

It beseeches me. Come, come, and

Release your tentative grip upon

This disappointing truth, your life.

Jump in with legs and arms waving

And drink me in; I wait on the edges,

Hovering and jeering. You will come.

I lean too far to the left, the right

And allow myself to plummet like

A bird who has forgotten to fly.

This homecoming, where death and

Unspent Possibilities

I sit clasping hands with charcoal

Thoughts. This is something I know.

Seven thirty in the room of horrors

I'm sorry I laughed, when we first approached the group,

And saw the motley conglomeration of lunatics within;

Forgetting, for a sweet free moment that I was one of them.

I am wrong for not understanding that this disease can crawl

In to the very hearts of those who refute it most, standing

Loudly in a circle of denial, grasping the last vestiges of hope.

I forgot that there are grades of madness, just like caste, a class,

Which mark us all out. Even here, in the hunched corners of

A moldering room, we sit with naked eyes and judge each other.

Unspent Possibilities

Two seasons in one year

Six months ago, we packed all the chunky woollens

In plastic packages, wrapped and tied with a sprig of hope

And placed them in the attic, out of sight, unnecessary.

We swapped the heavy blankets and many throws

For lighter sheets and spring-scented coverlets,

Opened the windows wide and waited. And waited.

We rose every morning with a tiny frisson of joy

Because surely, today, the sun would stream through

The blinds like a marathon runner reaching the last lap?

We slept heavily, still hibernating, watching and dreaming

And wondering when it would arrive, this fresh new season

Which everyone waits for, like a child sleeping for Christmas.

Jennifer Syrkiewicz

And now, as the frost hammers on the glass each morning,

And the leaves leap from the trees in suicidal arcs, we

Realise we were cheated; Stark slow winter is waiting again.

Unspent Possibilities

On Hope

I know, as the last warm blushed tendrils of light recede,

As darkness permeates everything, in my mouth, my nose,

As warmth fades leaving nothing but a stark black day,

That there is a monumental transformation taking place.

I have learned, if nothing else, lying along the tears, fear and

Seemingly everlasting evenings and sleepless dreams of

Death, that something will change. I have learned, once

And ever after, as sure as mathematics, that this, too, will pass.

Lament

Because I promised you, I will not open the packets

Of geometrically-spaced pills and let them dissolve on

My tongue like so many unsaid recriminations.

Because I promised you, I will not hide in this dark corner

And drink draughts of gin from the bottle, hoping to

Block out the angst-ridden scent of black clouded despair.

Because I promised you, I will not lay down to die among

The tattered failings of a ruined self. I will not listen to the

Logical voices of frantic pain and high self-loathing.

I will not drive our car in to a brick wall. I will not take a blade

Unspent Possibilities

And slash at the tender wrist-skin which bleeds like a bottle

Opening its mouth to release its poisoned sweet contents.

I will not crouch down under the weight of this sorrow which

Lets me know at every turn that I am heedless, nothing, blank

As an undrawn canvas waiting for a sad, lost tale to be told.

The oldest questions

A certain time in time, and so we stand,
Alone, we feel, with little left to say.
With nothing more than queries in our hands,
And very little light left to the day.
So long, these hours torn off the bigger sheet,
Ripped from the book which has planned out this page,
The smiles we take, the friends we will soon meet,
So quick to smile, or smart with sudden rage.
And yet beneath this thinly crumpled line,
A darker ink has spread like black-glazed night.
The pen will shed its innards, with a sign,
Expressing fear with every word it writes
There are no words to explain how to be,
Nor answers for those questions that we see.

Unspent Possibilities

My handful of cells

Not yet a you,

Yet you are –

A cell structure,

The meeting point.

The wriggling climactic climb.

The reason,

For self-discipline.

The topic of terror,

- and occasional joy -

and not drinking far too much wine.

A picture of red

Swimming frenziedly,

Naked as the day.

Beginning to grow

In limby spurts and pushes.

Far easier,

Less fraught -

As Moses, floating,

Perhaps would attest,

To be found in a basket of rushes.

Clinical Immunodermatology

She breathed through her skin. Mottled bumps and liquid shivers played across the surface of her arms, the light brown flesh attesting to her feelings more effectively than her impenetrable green eyes ever would. My foreplay, with her, was through speech. I could talk to her, my focus wholly on those two expressive limbs, and they spoke back to me with honesty, even as her mouth lied.

When I was frustrated with her, or confused, or lost, or simply wanted something to communicate with, I'd talk to her arms. They responded instantly, peaking in to orange-peel textures in reply to something which made her feel excited or enthusiastic. The tiny blonde hairs bleached by last season's sunshine would stand alert if I managed to find the right sentences to pique their imagination. Her arms preceded her, telling me how she felt about certain songs, or a flush of success, or the harrowing conclusion of a building thriller.

The rest of her was less interested in what I had to say. Over the course of our first few meetings she looked at me with a guarded expression, and it was only when I happened to glance down on our third or fourth encounter that I realised her flesh would communicate to me in a way she herself never would. And so it was, that I fell in love with one small part of the whole. Her arms. I think I loved her. In chance meetings, flushed, until she elbowed me away.

Jennifer Syrkiewicz

Send

Tapped characters, virtual sticks and curves

Half-formulated and pushed in to the ether

To clamber and bounce their way

Across a plump Monday morning.

Navigating clumsily past radio waves

And shadowed stills from films

And a telephone line over which

Two hushed voices proclaim undying love.

Past the burbled gimmicks of politicians

My broken characters dance, higgledy

And determined like sperm to the egg

Past raindrops, past falling leaves and rain.

They gather together, a regrouping regiment,

And jostle their way in to procession,

Unspent Possibilities

Climbing hastily in to binary rows

To punch out my greeting to you.

Jennifer Syrkiewicz

Transference

Suddenly very smart, and distant,

You sat with enigmatic eyes and

Smiled slightly, and couldn't hear

Until the weeping stopped again.

Think outside the box, and other clichés

You reminded me, and I looked out

At the haphazard snow and sighed.

I wondered what you would say if

I told you a truth, and unchecked it fell

In a straight line and landed on the floor.

I love you, I said, and you stared at me

For a gaping, stretched second, and

Then told me you shouldn't. Forgive me,

But when has that ever stopped a heart?

The days of the week on a chart, and

Unspent Possibilities

Each one embellished with honesty,

Reporting back between the lines of

Vicarious madness and slipped strength.

You enclosed, in the space you ask me

To think beyond, and now I won't heal.

You only like me when I'm broken.

Jennifer Syrkiewicz

Pause and think of me

Inside, with light struggling to prevail

Through fogged-up windows and old air,

With the clock unmoving and no sound,

I wait for you. I call.

In two-dimensional memory you smile,

And I grasp your bristled face in my hands,

And wonder if corporeal you

Can feel my embrace.

If this is so, you'll look up and turn

To face this dusty room where I lie,

And think of me, conjure my scent

From box files and cabinets.

Perhaps you'll pause and think of me.

Unspent Possibilities

Freud revisited

Contrary to unpopular belief,

Women do not malinger in

Bedrooms with crocheted

Throws, bemoaning the fact

That we do not have dicks.

And, just for the record, that

Half-marine scent? It comes

From you. Not us, from you.

And while it can be mentioned,

When wiring plugs, fixing shelves,

Mowing the lawn and all that jazz,

We do very well by ourselves.

If I am hysterical, forgive me. I

Think my womb is wreaking havoc.

Thorn Cross

He has my son, now.

I still get angry sometimes

And want to hit, and hurt.

I beat my conscience back

And watch the time roll slowly

Through the corridors and sunsets and

The broken glass.

Sometimes when memory plays a reel

Across my shuttered lids,

I see his face. He is hopeful, his brown eyes

Upturned in misguided trust, to me.

In another place, perhaps in death,

I hold his hand, looking down at him

And knowing I am a good man.

A good man. Not this. Not me.

Unspent Possibilities

You know who you are

Thank you for bringing me home

When I was running down the avenue

In my night dress and boots

Screeching like a banshee for the moon.

And thank you for holding my hand

When blood seeped through the

Wallpaper, running in tiny lines

On the clammy, stained restaurant floor.

And thank you for making me laugh

When all I wanted to do was crawl

Like a broken animal in to the safety

Of your arms. So warm. So safe and warm.

Jennifer Syrkiewicz

Everything still the same

With the fireworks of the midnight celebration

Still simmering stalks, memories of

Sparks flying above the snow-tipped roof

And the ringing of laughter echoing a mocking

Cadence, like being taunted.

With the crisp grey morning spreading recriminations

And the sickening tang of bile in a parched throat.

With the memory of words spoken too loudly,

Glasses dropped, cigarette ends scorching in to pile.

With all this, we look out beyond the passing of

The months, and resolve that this year, this year,

Things will be different.

www.ingramcontent.com/pod-product-compliance
Lightning Source LLC
Chambersburg PA
CBHW031217270326
41931CB00006B/589